COWS
ON THE FAMILY FARM

Chana Stiefel

Enslow Elementary

an imprint of

Enslow Publishers, Inc.

E

40 Industrial Road
Box 398
Berkeley Heights, NJ 07922
USA

http://www.enslow.com

CONTENTS

WORDS TO KNOW

breed—Type of animal in a group.

calf—A young cow.

graze—To feed on grass.

heifer (HEH fur)—A female cow.

herd—A group of cows.

PARTS OF A COW

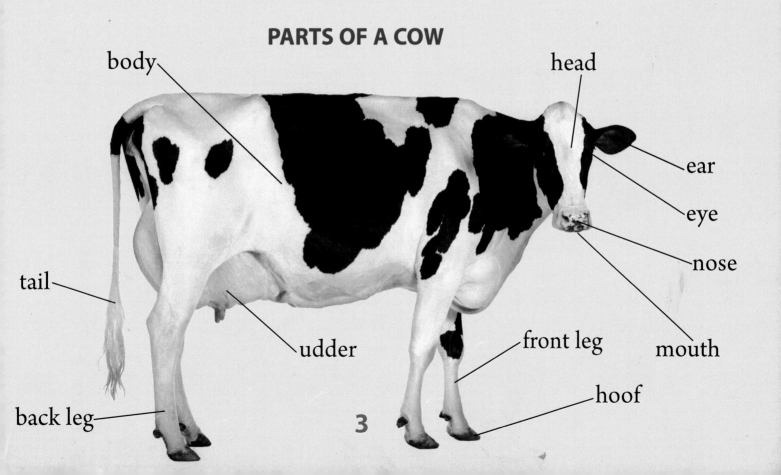

body

head

ear

eye

nose

tail

udder

front leg

mouth

hoof

back leg

3

WOW!

COWS!

Did you know that
a cow eats 50 pounds
of grass each day?
That's the weight of an
average second grader!
Find out more cool facts
about cows that live on
a family farm.

MEET THE
FARMERS

Matt raises eight dairy cows and about fifty cows for beef.

Matt and Tara raise cows and other animals on their family farm. The cows give milk to drink. The cows also give meat to eat. Matt and Tara's children, Jackand Alice, help on the farm, too.

Jack helps his family on the farm.

Grass is the cow's natural diet. Matt and Tara do not feed corn to their cows. A cow's stomach can digest grass very w

COW
CHOW

Matt and Tara's cows live in the fields all year. Most of the year, they eat grass. They also like other plants like herbs and clover. The cows eat and chew all day.

This cow enjoys some wild plants.

WINTER FOOD

Dry grass is called hay. It is an important food for cows during the winter.

In winter, the cows eat hay. Hay is dry, cut grass. Matt and Tara also feed their cows seaweed and sea salt. The cows need these foods to grow. When it snows, the cows keep each other warm. They move into the barn when icy rain falls.

Long hoses pump water into tubs for the cows to drink.

FOLLOW THE
HERD

The farmers gently walk behind the cows. They move the cows to a new field to **graze**. Jack and Alice give the cows buckets of water. Cows also drink water from big tubs.

Matt and Alice (on Matt's back) guide the cows to a new field.

CALVES
ARE BORN

In the spring, the cows give birth. Their babies are called **calves**. Newborn calves like to hide in the bushes. It is quiet there. Calves "moo" to their mothers. The mother cows "moo" back. Calves drink their mother's milk.

This is a newborn calf. Mom cleans the calf with her tongue.

Each cow gives about four gallons of milk a day. That's 64 cups each! The milk goes to people who live close to the farm. The milk you buy from the store comes from much bigger farms. Those cows are milked with large machines.

GOT MILK?

People also drink cows' milk. Matt gets up early to milk the cows. He brings the cows into the barn. Matt milks the cows by hand or with a "bucket milker." Milk is used to make butter, cheese, yogurt, and ice cream.

A bucket milker is attached to this cow. The milker gently pumps the cow's milk. The milk fills a bucket.

A Devon cow on the family farm has a healthy life.

SHARING AND
CARING

The family raises Devon cows for beef. People come to the farm to pick up the meat. They get dairy products, fruits, vegetables, grain, and eggs, too. "We are partners with nature," says Tara.

Matt, Tara, and Alice sell their healthy farm products to people in their town.

MANY DIFFERENT COWS

Not all cows are the same. There are different **breeds**. Some are good for giving milk. Some are better for beef. See how they look different?
Which is your favorite?

Jersey, milk

Ayrshire, milk

Holstein, milk

20

Hereford, beef

Devon, beef

Guernsey, milk

British White, beef

LIFE CYCLE OF A COW

1. A calf weighs 40 to 60 pound. A female calf is called a **heifer**.

3. A cow can weigh 1,000 pounds or more. A Jersey cow lives about 10 to 14 years. Some may live as long as 20 years.

2. A heifer is fully grown by its secor or third birthday. Then, it may giv birth to a new calf. Once a heifer gives birth, it is called a cow.

LEARN MORE

BOOKS

Doyle, Malachy. *Cow*. New York: Margaret K. McElderry, 2002.

Green, Emily K. *Cows*. Minneapolis, Minn.: Bellwether Media, 2007.

Macken, JoAnn Early. *Cows*. Pleasantville, N.Y.: Weekly Reader, 2010.

WEB SITES

Kids Farm. *Farm Animals*.
   http://www.kidsfarm.com/farm.htm

Smithsonian National Zoological Park. *Kids' Farm*.
   http://www.nationalzoo.si.edu/Animals/KidsFarm/IntheBarn

INDEX

Enslow Elementary, an imprint of Enslow Publishers, Inc.
Enslow Elementary® is a registered trademark of Enslow Publishers, Inc.

Copyright © 2013 by Chana Stiefel

Library of Congress Cataloging-in-Publication Data

Stiefel, Chana, 1968-
Cows on the family farm / Chana Stiefel.
    p. cm. — (Animals on the family farm)
    Summary: "An introduction to life on a farm for early readers. Find out what a cow
eats, where it lives, and when calves are born"— Provided by publisher.
Includes index.
    ISBN 978-0-7660-4205-6
    1. Cows—Juvenile literature. I. Title. II. Series: Animals on the family farm.
    SF197.5.S74 2013
    636.2—dc23
                                    2012028801

Future editions:
Paperback ISBN: 978-1-4644-0353-8
EPUB ISBN: 978-1-4645-1195-0
Single-User ISBN: 978-1-4646-1195-7
Multi-User ISBN: 978-0-7660-5827-9

Printed in the United States of America
012013 The HF Group, North Manchester, IN
10 9 8 7 6 5 4 3 2 1

To Our Readers: We have done our best to make sure all Internet Addresses in this book were active and appropriate when we went to press. However, the author and the publisher have no control over and assume no liability for the material available on those Internet sites or on other Web sites they may link to. Any comments or suggestions can be sent by e-mail to comments@enslow.com or to the address on the back cover.

Photo Credits: Howling Wolf Farm, pp. 4–5, 6, 7, 8, 11, 13, 15, 16, 19; © iStockphoto.com/Andrzej Sowa, p. 17; Shutterstock.com, pp. 1, 2, 3, 9, 10, 12, 14, 18, 20, 21, 22.

Cover Photo: Shutterstock.com

A note from Matt and Tara of Howling Wolf Farm: We grow vital food to feed individuals and families. Products include vegetables, beans and grains, dairy, beef, eggs, chicken, lamb, and pork. We work in partnership with nature and people to grow vibrant, abundant food. We farm with an intention of creating a farm and food to bring health, vitality, and enjoyment to our complete beings and the land. We focus on heirloom and open-pollinated varieties, heritage breeds, and wild foods.

Series Science Consultant:
Dana Palmer
Sr. Extension Associate/4-H Youth Outreach
Department of Animal Science
Cornell University
Ithaca, NY

Series Literacy Consultant:
Allan A. De Fina, Ph.D.
Past President of the New Jersey Reading Association
Professor, Department of Literacy Education
New Jersey City University
Jersey City, NJ